SONS OF ANARCHY

LIVE TO RIDE

RUNNING PRESS
PHILADELPHIA · LONDON

Books published by Running Press are available at special discounts for bulk purchases in the
United States by corporations, institutions, and other organizations. For more information, please
contact the Special Markets Department at the Perseus Books Group, 2300 Chestnut Street,
Suite 200, Philadelphia, PA 19103, or call (800) 810-4145, ext. 5000, or e-mail
special.markets@perseusbooks.com.

ISBN 978-0-7624-5517-1

Library of Congress Control Number: 2014939217

E-book ISBN 978-0-7624-5548-5

9   8   7   6   5   4   3   2   1
Digit on the right indicates the number of this printing

Cover and interior design by Jason Kayser
Edited by Jennifer Leczkowski
Typography: Brothers, Hawksmoor, and Ultramagnetic

Running Press Book Publishers
2300 Chestnut Street
Philadelphia, PA 19103-4371

Visit us on the web!
www.runningpress.com

"THE TRUE OUTLAW FINDS THE BALANCE BETWEEN THE PASSION IN HIS HEART AND THE REASON IN HIS MIND. THE SOLUTION IS ALWAYS AN EQUAL MIX OF MIGHT AND RIGHT."

IN 1967, upon returning from the Vietnam War, John Teller and Piney Winston founded the Sons of Anarchy Motorcycle Club in Charming, California. Inspired by a vision of freedom that operated outside the constraints of government and society, they created an organization that stands for the bond of brotherhood and liberation from authority. From the home base of the Mother Charter, the Sons of Anarchy Motorcycle Club, Redwood Original (SAMCRO), the legacy of John Teller and SOA lives on in his son Jax Teller, the club president, and the rest of the Reaper Crew. Protecting the livelihood of the club and the town of Charming and its people has always been SAMCRO's mission. However, Jax begins to question the direction of the club after discovering several of his father's journals and his manuscript entitled *The Life and Death of Sam Crow: How the Sons of Anarchy Lost Their Way*, which reveals the original manifesto for SAMCRO. Driven by his loyalty to the club and commitment to its legacy, Jax strives to steer the organization in a legitimate direction and find the balance that his father intended for the club, the "equal mix of might and right."

THIS IS ABOUT ONE OF US
THINKING STRAIGHT.

BRAINS
BEFORE BULLETS,
RIGHT?

—JAX

UNSER:

Charming's a special
town. Not many folks take
to it. I like to think the
town chooses its occupants.
Right ones stay.
Wrong ones disappear.

GEMMA:

I just want to
make sure he's following
in the right father's
footsteps.

ALVAREZ:
If you're here to declare war, consider it already on.

CLAY:
Him challenging me.
It's in his DNA.

CLAY MORROW

CLARENCE "CLAY" MORROW, the former president of SAMCRO, was a founding member of the club and Jax's step-father. The youngest member of the "First 9," Clay was a proponent of the gun running business in the U.S. and was instrumental in its operation in Charming. He was also the owner of the Teller-Morrow auto shop that he opened with John Teller, where the members of SAMCRO are employed. Following a unanimous vote, Clay was stripped of his patch and Jax became the new club president.

GEMMA:

You love the man.
You *learn* to love to club.
If you can do that,
there's no truth you
can't handle.

JUICE:
Take him out.
That means, like,
kill him?

CHIBS:
No, I think
what he means
is dinner
and a movie.

GEMMA:

Mommy moved away . . . or Mommy passed away. Your call.

JAX:

I'm not going to hurt you. I'm not going to hurt them. You don't have to run. Not anymore.

ANOTHER
MAGICAL DAY

TO BE ALIVE.

—UNSER

BOBBY MUNSON

ROBERT "BOBBY ELVIS" MUNSON is the former treasury secretary and vice president of SAMCRO. He is the even-tempered member of the group, and a sage counselor to Jax, though he doesn't hesitate to get violent when necessary. He is known as "Bobby Elvis" for his Elvis impersonations. Bobby resigned from the VP post after a disagreement with a club vote, but came back to SAMCRO after considering going Nomad. He loves SAMCRO and is a trusted and revered member of the club.

CLAY:

We got an obligation to
this club, this town,
to crush this threat.
Retaliation must be harsh
and immediate. That's what
we do. It's what we've
always done.

JAX:

Something happens at around 92 miles per hour. Thunder headers drown out all sound. Engine vibration travels at a heart's rate. Field of vision funnels into the immediate. And suddenly, you're not *on* the road, you're *in* it, a part of it.

HOME IS WHERE
THE
REAPER IS.

—BOBBY

JAX:

Hey, you want me to be
your number 2, protect this club,
then I gotta know where you're
taking us. Otherwise, there's
no trust. And if you and
me don't trust each other,
SAMCRO has got a problem.

JAX TELLER

JACKSON "JAX" TELLER is the current president and former vice-president of the Sons of Anarchy Redwood Original Motorcycle Club (SAMCRO). The son of John Teller (one of the founding members of the club, or "First 9") and Gemma Teller, Jax was raised in the club in Charming, California. While loyal to SAMCRO and his outlaw brothers, Jax begins questioning the club's principles after finding several of his late father's journals and an old manuscript. As the president of SAMCRO, Jax strives to steer the organization in a legitimate direction and leave a legacy for his sons Abel and Thomas.

LET'S RIDE.

CHIBS:

Listen, the rules have been
around since day one. Different time.
I'm not saying I agree with
them all. But you know, if I start
picking and choosing which ones
to follow then…the whole
thing just falls apart.

OPIE:

The outlaw had mercy.
You remember that
the next time you
try and twist the truth
to kill one of us.

JUICE:
Once you're patched the members are a family.
This charter is your home.

TARA:

I'll die if I have to. At least I know I tried to save them from becoming what you are.

CLAY:
Two in the back
of the head.
Quick and painless.

JAX:
It ain't easy
being king.

CLAY:
Yeah, you
remember that.

TARA KNOWLES–TELLER

TARA KNOWLES-TELLER was the wife of Jax Teller, the mother of his son Thomas, and step-mother to Abel. Previously high school sweethearts, Tara broke Jax's heart when she left Charming at age 19 to get away from small-town life and the influence of SAMCRO. She moved back to Charming after an 11-year absence and became a pediatric resident at the local hospital, St. Thomas. After officially becoming Jax's "old lady," Tara struggled to find acceptance of the activities of the club and reconcile her love for Jax and her need to protect her children from the life of SAMCRO.

You can't stop progress.
It won't be long before
SAMCRO's just an ugly memory
in this history of Charming.
So you enjoy the ride...
while you still can.

I'M A
COMPANIONATOR.

I BRING FOLKS
TOGETHER.

I'M ALL ABOUT THE
LOVE.

—NERO

TIG:

Jax is smart, and I appreciate his lead on a lot of stuff, but where we got to go now, it ain't about being smart.
It's about killing shit.

I GOT THIS.

—OPIE

WAYNE UNSER

WAYNE UNSER is the former Chief of the Charming Police Department. A longtime resident of Charming, he cares deeply for the town and its people. As Chief of Police, Wayne believed that the club was good for the town, keeping drugs out and protecting the population from gang violence. Now retired from the force and battling terminal cancer, Wayne lives in a trailer parked on the Teller-Morrow property, and continues to be a trusted friend and ally of SAMCRO.

JAX:
You want to be
an old lady?
Then act like one.
Do what you're told!

TARA:
I just helped you
kill someone.
That old lady enough
for you?

JAX:

I'm an okay
mechanic with a **GED.**
The only thing I
ever did well was
outlaw.

CLAY:

Don't go setting fires when there's nothing to burn. You hear me?

GEMMA:

I don't do that. Not all the time.

CLAY:

How do you want
to handle it?

JAX:

We kill 'em all.

JUICE ORTIZ

JUAN CARLOS "JUICE" ORTIZ is a member of SAMCRO and its hacker and intelligence officer. Originally from Queens, NY, Juice is of Puerto Rican descent and oversees surveillance, communication, and technology for the club. Regarded as unreliable by Clay, he was often given more menial tasks than the other members. Juice has committed a few club transgressions, though Jax has given him a second chance to show his commitment to the club. Juice continues to try and prove that his loyalty to SAMCRO has not wavered.

BOBBY:
Officer challenge.
Your leadership
is compromising this club.
I want a vote.
New president.

UNSER:

We wanna stay the same, but we can't. Older we get, the further away we get from who we think we are.

HE'S GOT TO DIE.

LIKE, A LOT.

—HAPPY

CLAY:
Maybe it's time to clean house.
Relationships are overrated.

JAX:

All in favor of Clay Morrow meeting
Mr. Mayhem?

CLAY:

Everybody at that table's done something that puts them outside the Reaper. Self-disclosure kills the group.

TIG TRAGER

ALEXANDER "TIG" TRAGER is a member of SAMCRO and its former Sergeant-at-Arms under Clay Morrow's presidency. As such, he was responsible for discipline within the chapter's jurisdiction and is the most violent member of the club. Known for his volatile personality, he has an affinity for strange activities and suffers from pediophobia (a fear of dolls). Tig was extremely loyal to Clay Morrow, and his strong loyal values have transferred to Jax as the new club president of SAMCRO.

JAX:

I never forced my
life on you. You came back
to me. You're part of
what I am, Tara, you
always have been.

CLAY:

Old ladies—they got a way of coming
back and biting you in the ass.

GEMMA:
He's not going down by law.
He's gonna die—by the hand of a son.

LIFE MOVES ON.
WE CHANGE.

≈

I HATE DIFFERENT THINGS NOW.

—GEMMA

JAX:
Call everyone.
Chapel.
We need
to take a vote.

HAPPY:

Oh yes I will!

GEMMA TELLER-MORROW

GEMMA TELLER-MORROW is the widow of John Teller and Clay Morrow and the mother of Jax Teller. She is the matriarch of SAMCRO and cares deeply for each member of the club. Born and raised in Charming, Gemma puts her town and her family above all else—at any cost. Her goal is to ensure the survival of SAMCRO for Jax and her grandsons Abel and Thomas.

JAX:

You know what, Mom?
I kind of have a few things on
my plate today. Like burying
my best friend. So your
need to be loved, worshipped,
and adored is a little low
on my list today.

CLAY:
You know, losing the gavel, I thought the shit I'd be jonesing for would be the money, the weight.

TIG:
Don't tell me it's about the brotherhood and the camaraderie or I'm gonna puke all over your goddamn table.

VULNERABILITY
IS A LIABILITY.

NO PLACE FOR IT
IN THIS LIFE.

—GEMMA

OPIE WINSTON

HARRY "OPIE" WINSTON was the son of Piney Winston, one of the founding members of SAMCRO. Jax Teller's best friend since childhood, Opie was also raised in the club, though he too sometimes had an ambivalent attitude towards the MC in his effort to reconcile club activities with the challenges of raising a family. He served a five year prison sentence, suffered the deaths of his wife and father, and ultimately sacrificed himself to a deadly beating in San Joaquin County Correctional Facility, all in the name of SAMCRO.

CLAY:

I've given my whole life to this club.
I don't want to walk away with nothing.

CHIBS:

Do you trust me, Jackie? Do you trust any of us? 'Cause it's not just your club.

Opie was right.
The gavel corrupts.
You can't sit in
this chair without being
a savage.

NERO:
My life's about
to get very
messy, Gemma.

GEMMA:
I know messy.
It's what I do best.

BOBBY:

When you want blind action, you go to Tig.
When you want the truth, you come to me.

CLAY:

See you on the other side.

CLAY:
So, I guess you,
uh, had
another vote
I wasn't privy to.

JAX:
Yeah, we did.
This time
it was unanimous.

CHIBS TELFORD

FILIP "CHIBS" TELFORD is the current vice president of SAMCRO. He is Scottish, though he grew up in Belfast, Ireland, and is a former member of the True IRA. He was the first prospect of the Sons of Anarchy Belfast Motorcycle Club (SAMBEL). Having been forced to leave Ireland by Jimmy O'Phelan, he patched over from SAMBEL to SAMCRO, becoming a liaison between the two charters. His experience as a medic for the British Army comes in handy as the club's backdoor emergency surgery medic. Nicknamed "Chibs" because of his facial scars ("chib" is Scottish slang for knife or slash), he is extremely loyal to Jax as VP of SAMCRO.

CLAY:

What kinda nasty shit did your momma do to you?

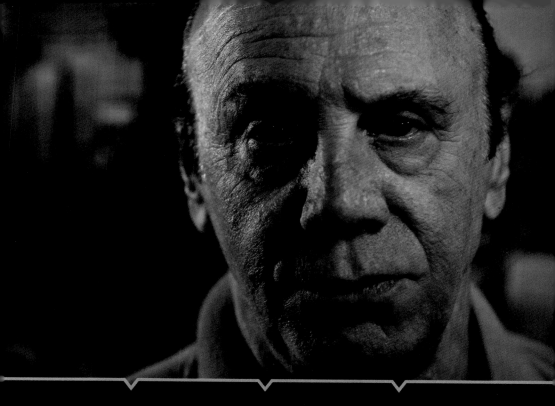

UNSER:

Come across something don't make you
miserable . . . enjoy it.

NOTHING HAPPENS IN

CHARMING

WE DON'T CONTROL OR GET A PIECE OF.

—CLAY

PINEY:

I don't know what the
hell's wrong with you.
Why don't you quit
whining, grow a dick, and
take care of your
business?

GEMMA:
My son loves deep . . .
hates deeper. It's
in our genes. Betrayal is
unforgivable.

CLAY:
Better to be safe
than stupid.

PINEY WINSTON

PIERMONT "PINEY" WINSTON was a founder of SAMCRO and father of Opie Winston. As one of the "First 9," he served as vice president under Jax's father, John Teller. JT and Piney served in the Vietnam War together and when they returned they formed SOA to create their own version of freedom. Piney served as vice president under Clay until Jax was old enough to take his place. After stepping down, Piney continued as a member, voting in club meetings to keep Clay in check (whom he didn't trust to lead SAMCRO), but rarely went on runs due to his emphysema.

TIG:
Are you
out of your
goddamn mind?

GEMMA:
Yeah,
maybe a little.

TARA:
You're not on borrowed time.
To me you're already dead.

CLAY:

We're not a gang, we're a motorcycle club.

TIME AND MONEY

FIXES EVERYTHING.

—CLAY

We all do damage.
Character is
determined by how we
repair it.

CLAY:

Nothing more
dangerous than a
guy who already knows
he's dead.

I'M TIRED OF BLOOD FOR BLOOD.

-JAX

HAPPY LOWMAN

HAPPY LOWMAN is the current Sergeant-at-Arms of SAMCRO. He was formerly a member of the Tacoma, Washington and Nomad charters before becoming a full patch with Redwood Original. A ruthless enforcer for the club, Happy is often tasked with the more violent jobs along with Tig. His name derives from his happy face tattoos that represent each of his assassinations. He replaced Chibs as Sergeant-at-Arms when Chibs was named Jax's vice president.

HE WENT OUT A
WARRIOR.

—JAX

CLAY:

You ever try to end run me through my old lady again, I'll slit your throat.

JAX:

Things are gonna get bloody, brother.

TIG:

I'm gonna dunk
my balls in your mouth.
You're gonna gag.
I'm gonna laugh.
We'll be best friends
forever.

JAX:

It's about me...
figuring out what I have
to do today that
keeps me
alive tomorrow.

★ ★ ★ ★ ★ ★ ★ ★ ★ ★ ★ ★ ★ ★ ★

YOU'RE ALL VERY UNBALANCED INDIVIDUALS.

★ ★ ★ ★ ★ ★ ★ ★ ★ ★ ★ ★ ★ ★ ★

—JAX